Discovering Religions

Judaism

Sue Penney

Heinemann Library
an imprint of Heinemann Educational Publishers
Halley Court, Jordan Hill, Oxford OX2 8EJ

MADRID ATHENS PARIS
FLORENCE PRAGUE WARSAW
PORTSMOUTH NH CHICAGO SAO PAULO
SINGAPORE TOKYO MELBOURNE AUCKLAND
IBADAN GABORONE JOHANNESBURG

First published 1987
This edition published 1995

99 98 97 96 95
10 9 8 7 6 5 4 3 2 1

British Library cataloguing in Publication Data
Penney, Sue
Judaism. – 2Rev.ed. – (Discovering Religions Series)
I. Title II. Series
296

ISBN 0 431 07390 2

Designed and typeset by Visual Image
Illustrated by Gecko Limited. Adapted into colour by Visual Image
Produced by Mandarin Offset
Printed and bound in China

Acknowledgements
Religious Studies consultant: W Owen Cole

Thanks are due to Rabbi Douglas Charing and Rabbi Arye Forta for reading and advising on the manuscript.

The author and publishers would also like to thank Rabbi Arye Forta for his help with the translations of scriptures.

The author and publishers would like to thank the following for permission to use photographs:
The Ancient Art and Architecture Collection p. 39; Werner Braun pp. 40 (top), 42 (top), 44; J Allan Cash Photo Library p. 32; Circa Photo Library pp. 12, 17; Bruce Coleman Ltd p. 25; A H Edwards/Circa Photo Library p. 13; Robert Harding pp. 6, 38; The Hutchinson Library p. 16; Jewish Education Bureau p. 8; The Jewish Museum p. 23; B Key/Christine Osborne Pictures p. 37; Peter Osborne p. 40 (below); Zev Radovan pp. 33, 34; Anat Rotem-Braun p. 21; Barrie Searle/Circa Photo Library pp. 11, 27, 29, 31; Juliette Soester pp. 10, 14, 18 (below), 28, 42 (below), 45, 47; The Weiner Library p. 36; Zefa pp. 7, 9, 15, 18 (top), 20, 22, 26, 46.

Cover photograph by Zefa.

The author and publishers would like to thank the following for permission to use material for which they hold the copyright:
The Assembly of Rabbis of the Reform Synagogues of Great Britain for the extracts from Reform services on pages 17 and 45 and the Israeli Declaration of Independence on page 39, which were published in *Forms of Prayer for Jewish Worship I*, 7th edition, 1977; Dalia Hardof Renburg for the Hamantaschen recipe, on page 23, which was published in *The Complete Family Guide to Jewish Holidays*, Robson Books, 1987; JNF Publishing Co. for the Hebrew alphabet, on page 13; Clive A Lawton for the Passover song, on page 27, which was published in *The Seder Handbook*, Central Jewish Lecture and Information Committee, The Board of Deputies of British Jews, 1984; Vallentine, Mitchell & Co. Ltd. for the extract from *The Diary of Anne Frank*, 1954, on page 37.

The publishers have made every effort to trace the copyright holders, but if they have inadvertently overlooked any, they will be pleased to make the necessary arrangements at the first opportunity.

Contents

MAP: where the main religions began

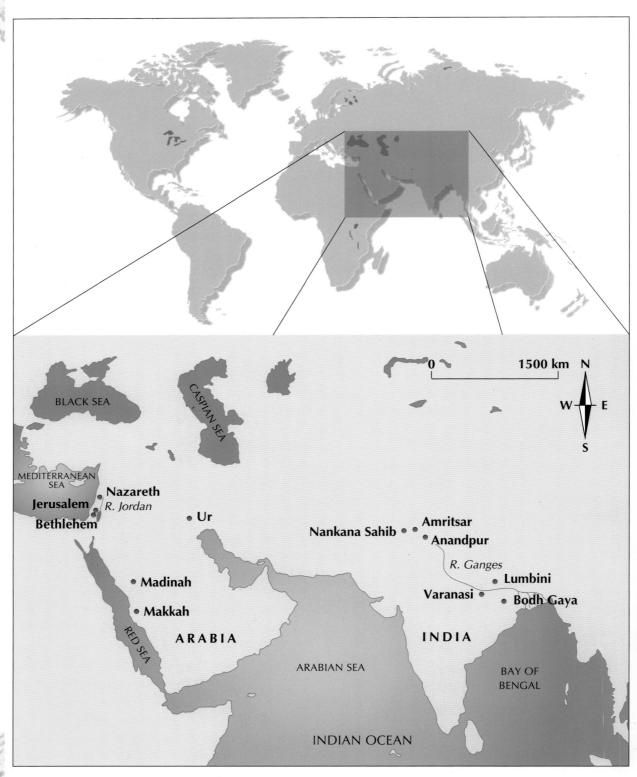

TIMECHART: when the main religions began

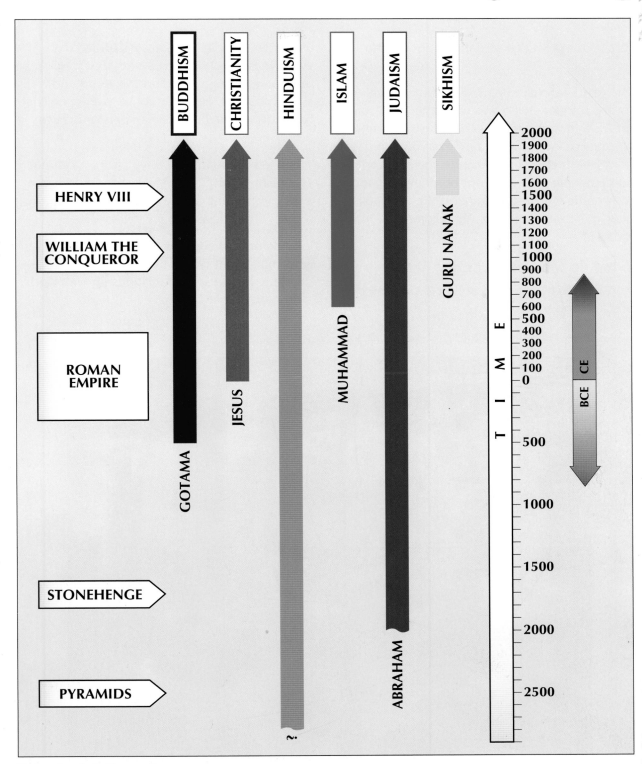

Note about dating systems

In this book dates are not called BC and AD which is the Christian dating system. The letters BCE and CE are used instead. BCE stands for 'Before the Common Era' and CE stands for 'Common Era'. BCE and CE can be used by people of all religions, Christians too. The year numbers are not changed.

Introducing Judaism

This section tells you something about who Jews are.

The word 'Jew' can be used in two ways. It means someone who was born a Jew. It also means a Jew who follows the Jewish religion, which is called **Judaism**. Not everyone who was born Jewish chooses to keep to the religion. Some people who were not born Jewish choose to become followers of Judaism. In this book, 'Jew' means a follower of the religion of Judaism.

What do Jews believe?

Jews believe that there is only one God, who is **eternal**. This means that he was never born and will never die. He is always present everywhere, and he knows everything. He made everything, including the world and everything in it. He cares about everything that he made and he listens when people pray to him.

When Jews pray to God, they call him **Adonai**. This means 'Lord'. Jews think that God's name is very important, so they use it with great respect. They never use it carelessly.

Jews do not believe that they are the only ones who know what God is like, but they do believe that Jews have a special relationship with God. They believe that God gave laws which they

This modern sculpture of a menorah is in Jerusalem

The Star of David is on Israel's flag

Temple was destroyed in 70 CE. It was the most important building in the Jewish religion.

The other symbol is a star with six points. This is called the Star of David, or sometimes the Shield of David. No one really knows where this symbol came from, but it has been used for hundreds of years. It is used as part of the flag of Israel, the country where many Jews live.

must obey. As long as they obey the laws, God will look after them. Their relationship with God is based on love. One of the prayers which Jews use most often shows how important this is. It says, 'You must love the Lord your God with all your heart, with all your mind and with all your strength'. This prayer is called the **Shema**.

Jewish symbols

Jews use many **symbols** in their religion, but two are especially important. One is the **menorah**. It is a candlestick which has seven branches. It reminds Jews of the lamps which were used in the **Temple** in Jerusalem. The

New words

Adonai name for God (means Lord)
Eternal lasting for ever
Judaism Jewish religion
Menorah seven-branched candlestick
Shema Jewish prayer
Symbol something which has a special meaning, or stands for something else
Temple most important place of Jewish worship (destroyed 70 CE)

The Shema

This is the first paragraph of the Shema.

Hear, Israel, the Lord is our God, the Lord is one. Now you must love the Lord your God with all your heart, and with all your soul and with all your strength. And these words, which I am commanding you today, shall be upon your heart. And you shall teach them carefully to your children, and speak of them when you are sitting in your house, when you are walking along the road, when you lie down and when you rise up. And you must bind them as a sign upon your arm, and they shall be a token between your eyes. And you must write them on the door posts of your house and on your gates.

Deuteronomy 6 : 4–9

The synagogue

This section is about the special place where Jews worship, and the things you find there.

A **synagogue** is the building where Jews go to worship God. The building is also used as the place where Jewish children are taught about their religion, and learn **Hebrew**. Hebrew is the language in which the Jewish **Scriptures** are written, so it is important for Jews to understand it.

Inside a synagogue

The most important thing in a synagogue is the **Ark**. This is a special cupboard, which is at the front of the main room. The **scrolls** are kept in the Ark. A scroll is like a book with one long page, which is unwound so that it can be read. The scrolls are very important, because the **Torah** is written on them.

Scrolls

A scroll is a long roll made of pieces of **parchment** stitched together. Parchment is made from animal skin which has been dried and smoothed so that it can be written on. The scroll has a wooden roller at each end, which the parchment is wound around. A scroll is about 60 metres long. Scrolls are written by hand, using special ink. The writing is in Hebrew. Scrolls are very important, and so they are looked after very carefully. The parchment is never touched with hands. When someone is reading from the scroll, a special pointer is used to follow the words.

Each scroll has a special cover which is used when it is put away in the Ark. The cover is called a **mantle**. It is usually made of silk or velvet. Mantles are often beautifully decorated with embroidery. Sometimes scrolls have other decorations, too. These are called the crown and bells. They help to remind people that the scrolls are important.

Inside a modern synagogue. (In this synagogue the women's section is upstairs)

Other important parts of the synagogue
The ever-burning lamp

In front of the Ark is a lamp in which the flame never goes out. This helps to remind people that God is always present. It also reminds Jews of the lamp which was in the Temple.

The Ark is at the front of the synagogue

The bimah

In the middle of the synagogue is a raised platform, which is called a **bimah**. The Torah is read from a table on this platform, and the person who is leading the service may stand there.

The women's section

In most synagogues, men and women do not sit together. Women have a separate section of their own.

The importance of the Torah

This story was told by Rabbi Jose the son of Kisma. It shows how important the Torah is to Jews.

Once, I was walking along the road when a certain man met me. He greeted me and I returned his greeting. He said to me, 'Rabbi, where are you from?' I said to him, 'I am from a great city of scholars and scribes.' He said to me, 'Rabbi, if you would be willing to live with us in our place, I will give you a thousand thousand gold coins, as well as precious stones and pearls.' I said to him, 'Even if you give me all the silver and gold and precious stones and pearls in the world, I would not live anywhere else but in a place where the people study the Torah. At the time when a man dies, neither silver nor gold nor precious stones nor pearls accompany him – nothing except the Torah he has studied and the good deeds he has performed.'

From 'The Sayings of the Fathers', Chapter 6 paragraph 9

New words

Ark cupboard which contains the scrolls
Bimah platform on which the reading desk stands
Hebrew Jewish language
Mantle cover for scrolls
Parchment writing surface made of animal skin
Scriptures holy books
Scroll roll of parchment on which the Torah is written
Synagogue Jewish place of worship
Torah Books of Teaching

Worship in the synagogue

This section tells you about how Jews worship in the synagogue.

For Jews, worship means praying to God, thanking him for the things he has done and asking for his help in their lives. They believe that worshipping God is very important.

Jews do not believe that they can only worship God if they are in the synagogue. They worship him in other places too. But every **Shabbat**, the Jewish holy day, many Jews go to the synagogue because it is a special place to worship God. As they go into the synagogue,

Jews wash their hands. This is not because they are dirty, it is a symbol to make them fit for prayer. Then they say a prayer which thanks God for the fact that they can worship him.

A synagogue service includes readings from the Scriptures, prayers and singing of **psalms**. (A psalm is a sort of poem.) Usually there is a talk called a **sermon**. Some synagogue services include readings from the Torah, the Books of Teaching which are written on scrolls. The scrolls are carried carefully from the Ark to the bimah to be read, and back again after the reading is finished. For a full synagogue service to be held, ten men must be present. If there

This boy is dressed for worship

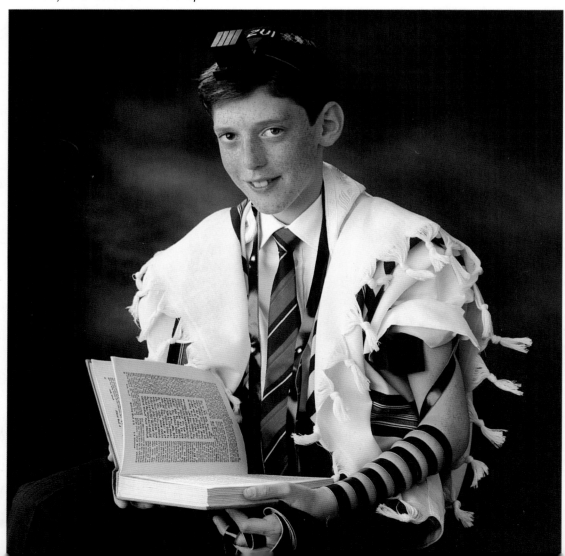

are not, the service will still be held, but not all of the prayers will be said.

Special clothes

At services in the synagogue, men wear a **kippah**. A kippah is a skull cap, which is often beautifully embroidered. It is worn as a sign of respect for God – many Jewish men wear one all the time. At morning services, they also wear a **tallit**. A tallit is a prayer robe, usually made of silk or wool. It has a fringe and tassels at the ends.

In Orthodox synagogues (see pages 40–1), men wear two small black leather boxes with straps as well as the tallit and kippah. These boxes are called **tefillin**. They contain small pieces of parchment. The parchment has short quotations from the Scriptures written on it. One box is worn in the middle of the forehead. This reminds Jews that they must love God with all their mind. The other is worn on the arm, facing the heart. This reminds Jews to love God with all their heart.

A tefillah (plural tefillin) with its contents

New words

Kippah skull cap
Psalm sort of poem, used like a hymn
Sermon special talk which teaches about religion
Shabbat Jewish holy day
Tallit prayer robe
Tefillin small leather boxes containing quotes from the Scriptures

Prayer on entering the synagogue

This is the prayer which Jews say as they enter the synagogue.

And I, due to your great kindness, will come into your house, and, in awe of you, I will worship facing towards your holy Temple. 'We will go to the house of God in a crowd'. How good are your tents, Jacob, your dwellings, Israel!

And I, due to your great kindness, will come into your house, and, in awe of you, I will worship facing towards your holy Temple.

Lord, I love the dwelling of your house and the place where your glory rests.

And I will worship and bow and bend my knee before the Lord my maker. And as for me, may my prayer come to you in an acceptable time; God, in your great kindness, answer me with the truth of your salvation.

Jewish holy books

This section tells you about the Jewish holy books.

The complete Jewish Scriptures are called the **Tenakh**. They are divided into three sections.

- Torah (The books of Teaching)
- Nevi'im (The books of the Prophets)
- Ketuvim (The 'writings')

Tenakh is a word made up of the first letters of these three names.

The Torah

The Torah is the most important part of the Scriptures. It contains the books called Genesis, Exodus, Leviticus, Numbers and Deuteronomy. For reading in the synagogue, these books are written on scrolls.

The word 'Torah' means teaching. The Torah is a group of books which teach Jews what God is like, and how they should live. They include the stories about the creation of the world and about the first Jews. They also include the rules about worship, festivals and the right ways to live. Altogether, there are 613 rules in the Torah. They are about all parts of life. Some Jews follow them more strictly than others. Some Jews follow them very closely, because they believe that it means they are living their lives in the way that God wants.

Another collection of teaching about how to live is called the **Talmud**. It contains the teachings of **rabbis**, collected together over many years and written down in about 500 CE. The Talmud gives much more detail about the Laws in the Torah, and helps to explain them.

Scrolls with their mantles and decorations

A scroll on the Bimah (notice the pointer, which is used when reading it)

Nevi'im

Nevi'im is a collection of books about the history of the Jewish people. It includes the teachings of the **prophets**. Jews believe that the prophets were men and women who had special powers given by God. This meant that they could tell people how God wanted them to live.

Some parts of Nevi'im are read in synagogue services. They are usually read from an ordinary book, not a scroll. Other parts of Nevi'im are not used in the synagogue, although Jews may read them at home.

Ketuvim

Ketuvim means writings, and most of the books contain stories from Jewish history. The book of Ketuvim which is used most often is the Book of Psalms. A psalm is a special poem, rather like a hymn. Psalms are often used in synagogue services.

New words

Prophet someone who tells people what God wants
Rabbi Jewish teacher
Talmud collected teachings of the rabbis
Tenakh Jewish Scriptures

Let's learn the Aleph-bet!

א **Aleph** – this letter is not sounded

ב With a dot it is **Bet** – pronounced 'B'
Without a dot it is **Vet** – pronounced 'V'

ג **Gimmel** – pronounced 'G' as in 'garden'

ד **Dalet** – pronounced 'D'

ה **Hey** – pronounced 'H'

ו **Vav** – pronounced 'V'
With a dot in the centre it is pronounced 'OO' as in 'hook'
With a dot on top it is pronounced 'AW' as in 'saw'

ז **Zayin** – pronounced 'Z'

ח **Chet** – pronounced 'CH' as in a Scottish 'loch'

ט **Tet** – pronounced 'T'

י **Yod** – pronounced 'Y'

ך כ With a dot it is **Kaph** – pronounced 'K'
Without a dot it is **Chaph** – pronounced 'CH' as in a Scottish 'loch'

ל **Lamed** – pronounced 'L'

ם מ **Mem** – pronounced 'M'

ן נ **Nun** – pronounced 'N'

ס **Samech** – pronounced 'S'

ע **Ayin** – this letter is not sounded

ף פ With a dot it is **Pey** – pronounced 'P'
Without a dot it is **Fey** – pronounced 'F'

ץ צ **Tsadi** – pronounced 'TS' as in 'let's'

ק **Kooph** – pronounced 'K'

ר **Resh** – pronounced 'R'

ש **Shin** – pronounced 'SH'

ש **Sin** – pronounced 'S'

ת **Tav** – with or without a dot, pronounced 'T' in modern Hebrew

The Hebrew alphabet

Shabbat

This section tells you about Shabbat, the Jewish day of rest and worship.

Shabbat is the Hebrew word for the Sabbath. It is the Jewish day of rest. It begins at sunset on Friday evening, and lasts until dusk on Saturday.

Shabbat is the oldest of the Jewish holidays. Jews remember the story in the book of Genesis about how God made the world. The story says that God worked for six days, and on the seventh day he rested. So Jews also rest on the seventh day of the week, which is Saturday.

Jews think that the Sabbath is very important. They believe that it is a special gift from God. It is a day of peace and rest. Jews look forward to the Sabbath all week. It is so special that it is sometimes called 'Queen Sabbath'.

Celebrating Shabbat

During Friday, the house is tidied and the table set, so that everything is ready to welcome the Sabbath. The Sabbath begins at sunset on Friday evening. It is always the wife or mother in a Jewish family who begins the Sabbath celebrations. The first thing she does is light two candles. As she lights them, she says a prayer which asks God to bless the home.

There is always a service in the synagogue on a Friday evening. When the family return home, the father blesses the children, and reads from the Scriptures. Then they all sit down at the table for the Sabbath eve meal. This is the most important meal of the week, and every family tries to make it the best they can afford. It is a relaxed, happy meal when families can enjoy each other's company, and Jews look forward to it from one week to the next.

The table is always covered with a clean white cloth, and the meal begins when the father recites a blessing called the **kiddush** over a cup of wine. Sabbath hymns are sung as the family sits at the table. The Sabbath meal often includes special foods, and there are always two loaves of bread. This is called **challah bread**, which is specially baked for the Sabbath. A blessing is said over the bread before it is eaten.

Lighting the Shabbat candles (notice the challah bread under its cover)

14

On Sabbath morning, many Jews go to the service at the synagogue. To make the Sabbath different from any other day, and to show how important it is, Jews must rest completely, and not do any work. Cooking is forbidden, so all food is prepared the day before. Strict Jews observe the rules very carefully, and – for example – will not drive or go shopping. It makes Shabbat a day which they can enjoy by relaxing together without feeling that there are things to do.

The Sabbath ends on Saturday evening, when the father says another blessing called the **havdalah**. A special plaited candle is lit, and everyone smells a special box of spices. The pleasant smell of the spices spreads through the house. Jews hope that this is a symbol of the way the peace and quiet of Shabbat will be remembered all through the coming week. After the blessing, the havdalah candle is put out by dipping it in a cup of wine. Shabbat is over when three stars can be seen in the sky.

The havdalah ceremony, with candle and spice box

New words

Challah bread special bread for the Sabbath
Havdalah blessing which ends the Sabbath
Kiddush blessing which begins the Sabbath

From the kiddush for Sabbath

God blessed the seventh day and pronounced it holy, for on it he rested from all the work which he had created to set the Universe in motion.

You are blessed, Lord our God, King of the Universe, who creates the fruit of the vine.

You are blessed, Lord our God, King of the Universe, who has made us holy with his commandments and has desired us and who, with love and goodwill, has made us inherit his holy Sabbath – a remembrance of the work of creation. For it is a day which is the beginning of all holy celebrations, a remembrance of the departure from Egypt. For you have chosen us and sanctified us from among all nations, and you have made us inherit your holy Sabbath in love and goodwill. You are blessed, Lord, who makes the Sabbath holy.

Rosh Hashanah and Yom Kippur

This section tells you about the important days at the time of the Jewish New Year.

Rosh Hashanah

Rosh Hashanah is the Jewish New Year. Jews have their own calendar, so New Year is not on 1 January. It falls in late September or early October. Jewish years are also numbered in a different way. They are 3761 years ahead of the Gregorian calendar which is used in most countries. For example, the Jewish year 5756 began in autumn 1995, the year 5761 will begin in 2000, and so on.

Rosh Hashanah reminds the Jews how God made the world. It is also the beginning of the most solemn time of the year. This lasts for ten days, which are called the Days of Returning. In these ten days, Jews think about the things they have done wrong in the past year. They make promises to themselves and to God that they will do better in the future.

The night before Rosh Hashanah, Jews have a meal at home. A special part of the meal is eating apples dipped in honey. This is a way of saying that everyone wishes that the year which is beginning will be sweet and pleasant.

A special synagogue service is held at Rosh Hashanah. The **shofar** is blown. A shofar is a ram's horn, hollowed out so that notes can be played on it. The notes it plays sound very solemn. They remind the people that God is very powerful, and they must listen to him.

Yom Kippur

Yom Kippur comes at the end of the Days of Returning. It is the Day of **Atonement**, which is the most solemn day of the year. Atonement means making up for something you have done wrong. It is a day when Jews pray to God to forgive them for the things they have done wrong.

Eating apples and honey

Blowing the shofar

New words

Atonement making up for something you have done wrong
Fast go without food and drink, often for religious reasons
Shofar ram's horn instrument

Prayer for the Days of Returning

This is part of a prayer used in Reform synagogues (see pages 40–1) during the Days of Returning.

The old year has died and the new year has scarcely begun. In this pause before the account is made of the past and my life is judged for what it is, I ask for honesty, vision and courage. Honesty to see myself as I am, vision to see myself as I should be and the courage to change and realize myself.

Your hand is open to every living being. At the smallest sign you come to meet us, for you are generous to forgive. On this day of repentance and return, stretch out your hand to me, so that I may grasp it, and lead me along the paths of love and duty into the harmony and peace which you have prepared for me.

At Yom Kippur, Jews **fast** for 25 hours. (This means they go without any food or drink.) They spend a lot of the day at the synagogue. They believe that if they are really sorry for the wrong things they have done God will forgive them. As well as praying for forgiveness, Yom Kippur is a day for remembering how kind God is, and how much he loves them. In the synagogue, the Ark and the reading desk are covered in white cloths, and the people leading the service wear white, too. This is a symbol to show that God has taken away the sins of the people who are sorry for what they have done wrong.

At the end of the service, the shofar is blown again. Its meaning is different from when it was blown at Rosh Hashanah. This time it reminds people that they must remember all the good things they have promised to do, and live good lives throughout the coming year.

Sukkot

This section tells you about Sukkot, the Feast of **Tabernacles**.

Tabernacle is an old word which means a sort of hut. The Hebrew word for this hut is **sukkah** (plural sukkot). The Feast of Tabernacles is the second festival of the Jewish year. In Hebrew it is called Sukkot. The festival lasts a week. Jews build a sukkah in the garden, and live in it for the week.

The Feast of Tabernacles celebrates two things.

- It recalls how the Jews in olden days used to take offerings of fruit to the Temple.

- It recalls how the Jews were once travelling in the desert and lived in tabernacles.

The most important part of the sukkah is the roof. This is made of branches, and has fruit

A sukkah

hung from it. It is built so that the sky can be seen through it. This is a reminder of the time in Jewish history when Jews were travelling in the desert with no proper home.

At the special synagogue service, everyone holds branches of certain trees – these are

Carrying the lulav and citron

called the 'lulav'. The trees are palm, willow and myrtle. The people hold the branches in their right hands. In their left hands they each hold a citron. A citron is a yellow fruit rather like a lemon. During the service, the people walk around the synagogue carrying these things. They also wave the branches. They are waved in all directions to show that God rules all the universe.

Each of the things they carry has a meaning. A sign or object that has a special meaning is called a symbol. The palm symbolizes the spine. The willow symbolizes the lips. The myrtle symbolizes the eyes. The citron symbolizes the heart. Joining them together reminds Jews that God must be worshipped with every part of them.

Simchat Torah

The day after the end of the Feast of Tabernacles is called Simchat Torah. This means the Rejoicing of the Torah. The books of the Torah are Genesis, Exodus, Leviticus, Numbers and Deuteronomy. They are very important for Jews. Parts of the books are read every week in services in the synagogue. During the year, the five books are read all through. At Simchat Torah, there is a special ceremony when the last part of the book of Deuteronomy is read, followed by the first part of the book of Genesis. Jews believe that the books show the way God wants them to live, so reading them like this is a way of showing that they should never stop following what God wants.

Simchat Torah is a very happy day. All the scrolls are taken out of the Ark and carried round the synagogue with the people dancing, singing and clapping after them. To celebrate the festival, children in the synagogue are given bags of sweets and fruit.

New words

Sukkah Hebrew word for tabernacle
Tabernacle sort of hut

How a scroll is made

A scroll is made of parchment, which is a special writing material made from animal skins. For a scroll, the animal must be kosher (see pages 42–3). The parchment is made in sheets which are stitched together. Traditionally, the threads used for stitching were tendons from the feet of a kosher animal. The ends are stitched round a wooden roller called the Etz hayim, which means 'tree of life'. The rollers are used to wind the scroll to the part which is to be read.

The writing on a scroll is in columns. A full Torah scroll has 250 columns. The writing is done by specially trained scribes, who write with special black ink using a quill pen made from the feather of a kosher bird. The writing must be perfect. If the scribe makes a mistake in a normal word, it can be rubbed out with a pumice stone, but if he makes a mistake in a word that refers to God, the piece of parchment must be carefully cut out and buried. (There are places in Jewish graveyards for this.) A patch is then stuck under the hole, and smoothed down so that the word can be re-written. It takes a scribe about 1000 hours to complete a full Torah scroll.

Hanukkah

This section tells you about the festival of Hanukkah.

Hanukkah is a winter festival. It usually falls in December, and it lasts for eight days. It is sometimes called the 'Festival of Lights'.

The story of Hanukkah

Hanukkah reminds the Jews of events that happened over two thousand years ago. It celebrates the bravery of a small group of Jews who were led by a man called Judah. His nickname was 'the hammer'. In Hebrew, hammer is 'maccabee' so he is called Judah the Maccabee.

Lighting the hanukiah

Judah was the leader of a small group of men who were fighting for what they believed. Their country had been taken over by an enemy. The new ruler was called Antiochus. He would not let the Jews worship their own God. He said that they had to worship him! The Jews knew that Antiochus was only a man, and it would be wrong to worship him.

Judah and his small group of friends fought against the cruel emperor Antiochus for three years. At last they managed to beat his army in a battle. The battle was important, because it meant that they had captured Jerusalem. Jerusalem is a very important city for the Jews. The Temple was in Jerusalem, and the Temple was the most important building in the Jewish religion. Antiochus had tried to spoil the Temple, so that Jews could not use it. He had ordered that a pig should be killed on the altar, one of the most important parts of the Temple. This made the Temple unclean – far worse than just dirty. It could not be used to worship God again until it had been specially cleaned and made holy again.

After Judah had captured Jerusalem, one of the first things he did was give orders that the Temple should be made fit to worship God again. When the Temple was ready, the menorah was lit. This was the Temple lamp, which had seven branches. The menorah was supposed to burn all the time, but Antiochus had let it go out. When it was re-lit, Judah's men discovered that it only had enough oil in it to burn for one night. They went to fetch more, but the oil was special, and it took eight days to get it. When the soldiers got back, the lamp was still alight. The people said that this was a **miracle**. God had made the lamp burn even though it did not have enough oil. This showed that he was pleased that the Temple had been made fit to worship him again.

Playing the dreidle game

Celebrating Hanukkah

When they celebrate the festival today, Jews use a special candlestick in their homes. It is called a **hanukiah**. It is a candlestick with eight branches and an extra holder for the 'servant candle' which is used to light all the others. One candle is lit on the first night of the festival, two on the second night, and so on. Each one is lit using the ninth candle. Before each candle is lit, special prayers are said. By the end of the festival, all nine candles are burning. Some Jews burn olive oil instead of candles, so that it is more like the miracle in the Temple.

Hanukkah is a very happy festival, especially for children. They go to parties and give each other presents. There is a special game which children play at Hanukkah using a four-sided top called a **dreidle**. On each side of the dreidle there is a Hebrew letter. The letters are the first letters of the Hebrew words which say 'A great miracle happened here'.

New words

Hanukiah candlestick with eight branches
Dreidle four-sided top
Miracle event which cannot be explained

How to play the dreidle game

■ Make or buy a four-sided spinning top.

■ On each side, paint one of the Hebrew letters:

Nun ‎נ‏   Hey ‎ה‏

Gimmel ‎ג‏   Shin ‎ש‏

■ Have ready a 'bank' of sweets, nuts or counters in the middle of the table.

■ Spin the dreidle.

□ If Nun comes up, this means you take nothing.

□ If Hey comes up, you take half the sweets.

□ If Gimmel comes up, you take all the sweets.

□ If Shin comes up, you put sweets back in to the 'bank'.

■ The game goes on with pl[...] adding to the 'bank' if it emp[...] until a player taking all the s[...] declared the winner.

Purim

This section tells you about the festival of Purim.

Purim is a very exciting festival, especially for children. It takes place in February or March. Purim tells the story of a good queen and a bad man. The story is in the Jewish Scriptures and in the Bible. It is called the Book of Esther.

The story of Purim

Esther was the name of the good queen. The bad man was called Haman. They lived a long time ago in a country called Persia. Haman was the King's Chief Minister in the government. He had quarrelled with a Jew who refused to bow as Haman passed. Bowing is a sign of worship, and Jews believe that it is wrong to worship anyone except God. Haman disliked the Jews, and because he was so angry he made a plan to kill all the Jews in Persia. To do this, he had to get the king to order the killings. Haman went to the king and told lies about the Jews. The king agreed that all Jews in the country should be killed. Haman could not make up his mind on which day the killings should be carried out, so he decided to draw lots. Purim is a word for 'lots', and this gives the festival its name.

Queen Esther heard about this. Although the king did not know it, she was Jewish. She decided that the Jews must be saved. The only way this could happen was if she could persuade her husband – the king – to change

A play for Purim

This scroll of the Book of Esther is in the Jewish Museum in London

his mind. This was a dangerous thing to try to do – she was only supposed to go to see the king when he sent for her! She was very brave. She invited the king and Haman to a feast. During the meal she told her husband the real reason why Haman wanted to kill all the Jews. The king was very angry. He ordered that Haman should be killed, and all the Jews were saved.

Celebrating Purim

At the Festival of Purim, the story of how all this happened is read out in the synagogue. Every time the children hear the name of Haman, they make as much noise as they possibly can. They hiss and stamp their feet. They use special rattles (called **greggors**) and whistles. The idea is to make so much noise that Haman's name cannot be heard at all.

At Purim, children often go to fancy dress parties. Sometimes they put on special plays at school or in the synagogue to show the story. In Israel there are plays and carnivals in the streets. Purim is also a time when Jews give money to charity, and give gifts of food to each other. This makes sure that even poor people can celebrate the festival with a special meal.

New word

Greggor rattle used by children at Purim

Hamantaschen

Hamantaschen – 'Haman's purses' – are a traditional food at Purim.

Pastry	Filling
12 oz plain flour	2 tablespoons milk
4 oz sugar	2 tablespoons honey
1 teaspoon baking powder	2 oz sugar
1 egg, beaten	4 oz poppyseeds
4 oz margarine, creamed	2 oz walnuts teaspoon lemon juice
2 tablespoons orange juice	grated rind of $\frac{1}{2}$ a lemon

Make the pastry: Sieve together the flour, sugar and baking powder. Mix the egg, margarine and juice. Add the two mixtures together. Refrigerate for several hours. Roll out to 3mm thickness, and use a 6cm cutter to cut into rounds.

Make the filling: Boil the milk, honey and sugar together. Add poppyseeds and cook for 5 minutes. Add other ingredients and cook until mixture thickens.

Make the Hamantaschen: Cool, and then put $\frac{1}{2}$ teaspoon of filling in the centre of each round. Pinch the pastry together to make triangle 'purses'. Pre-heat the oven to 180°C, place the pastries on a greased baking tray and cook for 10–12 minutes until golden. Cool on a wire tray.

Pesach

This section tells you about the story of Pesach, the Feast of Passover.

Passover is the most important Jewish festival. It celebrates something that happened nearly 4000 years ago. In those days, the Jews were living in Egypt. The king of Egypt was called the **Pharaoh**. The Pharaoh had made the Jews slaves. Their lives were very difficult. They had to work very hard, and were very badly treated. They had to build enormous storehouses for the Pharaoh. He had special slave-drivers to make them work hard. If they did not work fast enough – or if the slave-drivers felt like it – they were beaten with whips.

One of the Jews was a man called Moses. God spoke to Moses, telling him that he was to rescue the Jews. He went to the Pharaoh and said, 'Let my people go!' The Pharaoh refused, but then a series of disasters happened in Egypt. They are called **plagues**. Everyone believed that these plagues had been sent by God. Flies, frogs, locusts, cows dying ... altogether there were ten plagues. Each time there was a plague, the Pharaoh said that the Jews could go. As soon as the plague ended, he changed his mind and said that they must stay. The last plague was the most terrible. The eldest son in each Egyptian family died. God warned Moses that this would happen. He told Moses to tell the Jews to put lambs' blood on the doorposts of the Jewish houses. Then the Jewish boys would not die.

The ten plagues

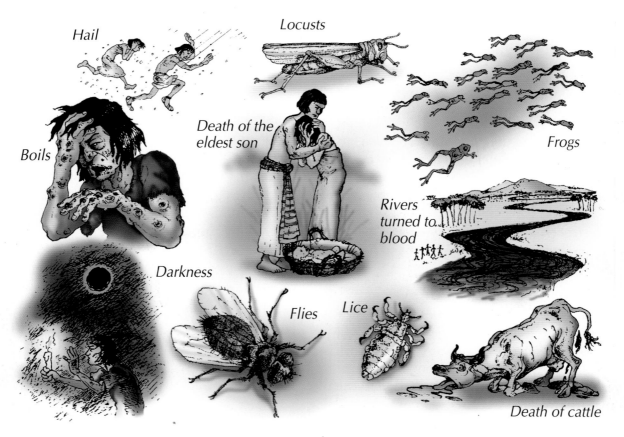

Hail

Locusts

Death of the eldest son

Frogs

Boils

Rivers turned to blood

Darkness

Flies

Lice

Death of cattle

The Pharaoh was so upset by the death of the boys that he said the Jews really could go. They prepared to leave as quickly as they could. They needed food for the journey, but there was no time to wait for the yeast to rise in the bread which they made. It was baked as it was. Although he had said they could leave, the Pharaoh changed his mind again. He sent his army after the Jews to bring them back. They were saved because of the water in the Sea of Reeds. It parted to allow them to cross. As soon as the Egyptian army tried to follow them, the sea flooded back and the Egyptians were drowned.

Passover reminds the Jews of three things.

- God is good – he helped his people.

- Death 'passed over' the houses of the Jews.

- The Jews passed over the Sea of Reeds when they were leaving Egypt.

One of the plagues was a swarm of locusts

New words

Pharaoh king of Egypt

Plague disaster sent by God

Keeping the Passover

This quotation from the Book of Exodus tells how Moses told the Jews to keep the Passover.

> *Remember this day as the time when you departed from Egypt, from the house of slavery, when the Lord took you out of here with his great power – nothing leavened may be eaten. For seven days you shall eat matzot, and the seventh day will be a festival for the Lord. Matzot must be eaten for the seven days and neither anything leavened nor any yeast must be seen in your possession throughout all your territories. And on that day you must explain to your children why you are doing this, saying to them, 'The Lord did wonders for me when I went out of Egypt so that I could carry out these commandments'. And the commandments shall be written as a sign bound onto your hand and a memorial placed on your forehead, so that the Torah of the Lord should become part of your everyday conversation, for the Lord brought you out of Egypt with his great power. And you must observe this practice at its proper time, year by year.*

Exodus 13 : 3, 6–10

Celebrating Pesach

This section tells you how Jews celebrate Pesach, the Feast of Passover.

Passover takes place in late spring. Before the festival begins, the house is cleaned. Any **leaven** is removed. Leaven is anything like baking powder or yeast which makes dough rise. This is a reminder that when the Jews were leaving Egypt there was no time for the bread to rise. On the night before the festival begins, the house is searched. Any tiny piece or crumb of leaven is swept up with a feather and burned. Nothing which contains leaven is eaten during the festival.

The Seder

The main part of the Passover celebration is a meal. This is called the **Seder**. The Seder meal follows a special 'order' which is written down in a book called the **Hagadah**. The Hagadah tells the story of the slavery and how the Jews left Egypt. The story is told as the meal is eaten. The youngest child present at the meal asks four questions. The questions are answered as the family read the story. In the answers to the questions, the person leading the meal talks about the things on the Seder plate. This is a special plate divided into five sections. Each

section contains a special food. The foods are symbols which remind the Jews of the slavery and how they left Egypt.

Special foods for the Seder

- Shank bone – not eaten, but a reminder of the lamb which was killed so its blood could be put on the doorposts.

- Egg – hard-boiled, then roasted in a flame. A reminder of the animals which used to be **sacrificed** in the Temple, and a symbol of new life.

- Green vegetable – usually parsley or lettuce. A symbol of the way God cared for the Jews when they were travelling in the desert.

- Bitter herbs – usually horse-radish. A symbol of the bitterness of slavery.

- Charoset – a sweet mixture of apples, nuts, spices and wine. A reminder of the 'cement' used by the slaves when they were building, and a symbol of the sweetness of freedom.

There are three other important things on the table.

The Seder meal

The Seder plate with matzot (plural of matzah)

- A bowl of salt water, which is a symbol of the tears of the slaves. The parsley or lettuce is dipped in this.

- A glass of wine for each person. Wine is drunk four times during the meal. This is a reminder of the four promises which God made to Moses.

- **Matzot**, which are flat 'cakes' of unleavened bread. These are a reminder of the bread which did not rise.

Not everything eaten at Passover has a meaning. The Seder also includes a 'proper' meal. At the end of the Seder, the family stay at the table and sing songs. Many have repeated words or phrases, which even very young children can enjoy joining in.

Passover reminds Jews of their history, and of how Jews have suffered more recently. It helps them to look forward to a time of peace and joy. The last words of the Seder are:

Next year in Jerusalem,
Next year may all be free.

New words

Hagadah book in which the Seder is written
Leaven yeast, baking powder, etc.
Matzot unleavened bread
Seder special Passover meal
Sacrifice offering made to a god

A Passover song

Many songs are sung at Passover. This one has been translated to fit the tune of 'Green grow the rushes, Oh!'

> *Who knows what one is, now our Seder's finishing?*
> *I know what one is:*
> *One is God for evermore on earth and up in heaven.*

The verses count through to thirteen like this.

> *Two are the stones of Law on which the Cov'nant's given,*
> *Three are the Fathers of the Jews,*
> *Four are the People's mothers,*
> *Five are the books of the Torah,*
> *Six are the sections of Mishnah,*
> *Seven are the days in ev'ry week,*
> *Eight is the day to circumcise,*
> *Nine are the months of pregnancy,*
> *Ten are the commandments,*
> *Eleven are the stars in Joseph's dream,*
> *Twelve are the tribes of Israel,*
> *Thirteen virtues God displays.*

Shavuot

This section tells you about Shavuot, the Feast of Pentecost.

The Feast of Pentecost is held seven weeks after the Feast of Passover. This is why it is sometimes called the Feast of Weeks. In Hebrew its name is Shavuot. It celebrates the Jews' belief that God gave the Ten Commandments to Moses.

Before the festival begins, the synagogue is decorated with fruit and flowers. This is often done by the children. It reminds people of how Mount Sinai bloomed with flowers when God came down to give the Torah to Moses.

Celebrating Shavuot

The festival begins with a service in the synagogue. This includes the reading from the Scriptures about how God gave the Ten Commandments to Moses. The Ten Commandments are a set of rules about how to live. Jews believe that they were given to Moses when the Jews were travelling in the desert after they had left Egypt. Jews believe that this is the most important thing that has ever happened to human beings, because it was God telling people how he wanted them to live.

Synagogues are decorated for Shavuot

Many of the Ten Commandments are quite long, but the rules they give can be summed up like this.

1 I am the Lord your God. You must not have any other gods but me.

2 You must not make any **idols** to worship.

3 You must not use God's name carelessly.

4 Remember to keep the Sabbath day holy.

5 Respect your father and your mother.

6 You must not murder.

7 You must not commit **adultery**.

8 You must not steal.

9 You must not tell lies about other people.

10 You must not **covet**.

After the synagogue service, there is a festival meal at home. Part of the meal is two special loaves of bread. They are decorated with a ladder pattern. This reminds Jews of how Moses climbed Mount Sinai to talk to God and be given the Ten Commandments.

Ladder bread

New words

Adultery sexual relationship outside marriage
Covet be jealous of what someone else owns
Idol false god (often a statue)

Receiving the Ten Commandments

This passage tells what happened when God gave the Ten Commandments to Moses.

> *Now as morning broke on the third day, there was thunder and lightning, and a heavy cloud hanging over the mountain, and the sound of the shofar grew very loud, and all the people who were in the camp trembled. Then Moses led the people out from the camp to meet God; and they positioned themselves at the foot of the mountain. By now, Mount Sinai was full of smoke because the Lord had come down upon it in fire; and its smoke rose up like the smoke of a furnace, and the whole mountain shook terribly. Then the sound of the shofar grew louder and louder; Moses spoke, and God answered him in a powerful voice. So the Lord came down on Mount Sinai, on to the top of the mountain; and the Lord summoned Moses to the top of the mountain, and Moses went up.*

Exodus 19 : 16–20

Jewish history

This section tells you something about Jewish history.

Jewish history began about 4000 years ago in the part of the world that today we call the Middle East. No one person ever 'began' Judaism. The beliefs that became the Jewish faith came about gradually. However, some people were important in making it happen.

One of the most important men was called Abraham (see pages 32–3). He was the first to believe that there was only one God. He left his home and went on a long journey, because he believed that was what God wanted him to do. God showed him the way to a new country called Canaan. God promised Abraham that one day his descendants would possess this country. This is the reason it is sometimes called the Promised Land.

After Abraham, the next great leader was a man called Moses (see pages 34–5). He lived about 500 years after Abraham. When Moses was alive, the Jews were slaves in Egypt. Moses became their leader and rescued them from slavery. These are the events which are remembered at Passover. After they left Egypt, the Jews lived in the desert for about 40 years. Then they settled back in Canaan again.

Jews lived around that area for hundreds of years, although the country's name and its borders changed many times. For most of the time, they were ruled by kings. One of the most famous kings was David. He lived about 3000 years ago. When David became king the country was very small and very poor, and the government was badly organized. David changed all that. He ruled well, and the country became rich and respected.

Other people who played an important part in the history of the country were not part of the government. They were called prophets. A prophet is someone who tells people what God wants. Sometimes they told kings too! Some of the prophets were important people in the country. Others were ordinary men and

Historical map of the Middle East

Jews today come from all parts of the world (this boy comes from Ethiopia)

about 2600 years ago. He was sure that God wanted him to warn the people that the way they were behaving was wrong. He told them that it would lead to the country being destroyed by an enemy. The people did not like being told this, and Jeremiah was very unpopular. He was put in prison, and people tried to kill him. Even though he did not want to carry on preaching, he felt he had to. He said that God's message was like 'a fire burning inside him'. His words came true in 598 BCE when Jerusalem was taken over by invaders from a place called Babylon.

During their history, the Jews' country has been taken over several times. Other nations ruled over them. Sometimes Jews were taken away from their own land and made to live in their enemy's country. Other Jews left by choice, because they did not want to live being ruled over by their enemies. They went to find a new life somewhere else. This is one of the reasons why today there are Jews all over the world.

women. They all felt that God was telling them what to do and say.

One of the most important prophets was a man called Jeremiah. He lived in Jerusalem

Choosing a Prophet

This passage tells how God chose the prophet Jeremiah.

And the word of the Lord came to me, as follows,
'Before I formed you in the womb, I knew you,
and before you were born I made you holy –
I have appointed you to be a prophet to the nations.'
But I said, 'But, Lord God, look, I do not know how to speak, for I am still young.'

Then the Lord said to me,
'Do not say "I am still young",
for everywhere I send you, you will go,
and everything I command you, you shall speak.
Do not be afraid, for I am with you to take care of you.'

Jeremiah 1 : 4–8

Abraham

This section tells you about the first founder of Judaism.

Judaism did not suddenly 'begin'. It developed gradually, and came about through many different people. One of the first and most important of these people was a man called Abraham. He is often called one of the 'fathers' of Judaism.

Abraham lived about 4000 years ago in a town called Ur. Ur was in the part of the world that today we call Iraq. It was a very splendid city. It had gardens and tall buildings. Abraham was rich and respected. He and his wife Sarah had servants and lots of sheep and camels. In those days, the number of animals someone owned showed how rich they were.

The people of Ur worshipped many gods. There were gods of the sun, the moon and the stars. Their worship included many things which Abraham began to see were wrong. For example, they were worshipped with human sacrifices. This means that people were killed so that their life could be an offering to the gods. Abraham began to think that there was one God who ruled everything. He was more important than all the other gods. Gradually, Abraham became more and more sure about this 'true' God. He also became sure that God did not want to be worshipped in evil ways.

Abraham felt that God was telling him to leave Ur and travel to another country. He and his family set out. They did not know where they were going, but they believed that God would show them the way to go. In those days, people often moved around from place to place, because they needed to search for water for their animals. This is called being a **nomad**. Abraham's journey was different, because he felt he was being guided by God.

As they travelled, Abraham felt that he was getting to know more about his God. He felt that a special relationship was beginning. Jews

Moon gods in Ur were worshipped in ziggurats like this

These nomads still live in much the same way as Abraham did

believe that God promised Abraham that he would become the father of a great nation. All his children and their children for ever would have this same special relationship with God.

Instructions to Abraham

This is how the Bible describes what God told Abraham to do.

> *Now the Lord said to Abraham, 'Go away for your own good – away from your country, the place you were born and your father's house – to the land which I will show you. And I will make you a great nation; I will bless you and make your name great, and you will become a blessing. I will even bless those who bless you, and anyone who curses you I will curse; and all the families of the earth will be blessed through you.'*

When Abraham reached the place that God had told him about, God said,

> *'Raise your eyes, and from where you are standing, gaze towards the north and the south, towards the east and the west. For I shall give all the land which you see to you and your descendants for ever. And I will make your descendants as numerous as the dust of the earth; so that if anyone will be able to count the dust of the earth, so your descendants will be counted.*

Genesis 12 : 1–3; 13 : 14–17

33

Moses

This section tells you about Moses.

Moses was the second great leader of the Jews. He lived at a very difficult time in Jewish history. For many years, the Jews had been slaves in Egypt. They were treated with great cruelty by their Egyptian masters. The Egyptians were afraid that the Jews might try to take over the country, so they decided that they must get rid of all Jews in Egypt. As part of this, they ordered that all baby boys should be killed at birth. Moses was not killed, because his mother hid him in a basket by the side of the river. He was found by the Pharaoh's daughter. She took him back to the palace and brought him up as if he were her own son.

When Moses grew up, he saw that the Jews were being very badly treated. One day he lost his temper and killed a slave-driver who had beaten a Jew to death. Then he had to leave Egypt, or he too would have been killed. He stayed away for several years, but gradually he became sure that God had work for him to do. God spoke to him, telling him to go back and get the Jews freed from slavery. At first he tried to make excuses to God about not going back, but at last he did. The Pharaoh did not want to let the Jews go, but a series of disasters (plagues) happened in Egypt. Moses told the Pharaoh that these plagues were sent by God, and at last the Pharaoh agreed to free the Jews.

The Jews' troubles were not over even after they had left Egypt. They spent the next 40 years wandering from place to place. They were nomads. These are called the years in the **wilderness**. A wilderness is like a desert where not very much grows. Eventually they found their way to the country called Canaan, and this became their home.

During the years when they were wandering, Moses was the Jews' leader. Jews believe that whilst they were in the wilderness, God gave Moses the Torah, the Teaching which Jews follow. This Teaching is very important for Jews, because it is part of their agreement with God. This agreement is a very serious one. It is called the **Covenant**. God promised that the Jews

This Egyptian painting shows the Jews as slaves

The life of Moses

would be his 'Chosen People'. This does not mean that they would be his favourites. It means that they were chosen to be given extra responsibilities. God would look after them but, in return, the Jews must obey the laws which God gave.

In Jewish history, this is remembered as God's second promise to the Jews. The first promise was to Abraham – God promised that Abraham would be the father of a great nation. The second promise was to Moses – God would take special care of the Jews, if they obeyed his laws.

New words

Covenant solemn agreement
Wilderness place where little grows

The Covenant

This passage tells how God told Moses about the Covenant.

> And the Lord said to Moses, 'Write these words for yourself, for according to these words I have made an agreement with you and with Israel.' And he remained there with the Lord for forty days and forty nights; he neither ate bread nor drank water, and he wrote the words of the agreement on stone blocks – ten statements.
>
> Then when Moses came down from Mount Sinai – the two blocks of the testimony being in Moses' hand as he came down from the mountain – Moses did not know that the skin of his face was still shining from when God had spoken to him. And Aaron and all the Israelites looked at Moses, and saw the skin of his face shining, and they were afraid to approach him. But Moses summoned them and taught them all the words which the Lord had spoken to him on Mount Sinai.

Exodus 34 : 27–32

Persecution

This section tells you about how Jews have been punished for their faith.

Persecution means being punished for what you believe. Jews have been among the most persecuted people in history. No one has ever been able to explain why this is so. The most likely reason is that Jews have been misunderstood. For example, Jews believe that they are God's 'chosen people'. Sometimes non-Jews have thought that this means that Jews feel they are better than other people.

Keeping their own religion and customs is very important for Jews. This has been the only way that their religion has survived. Sometimes this was seen by other people as being dangerous or threatening. It meant that Jews were 'different', and people are often afraid of what they do not understand. Sometimes, customs were really misunderstood. In other cases, they were deliberately 'twisted' so that Jews could be accused of things they had not done. In the Middle Ages, Jews were often persecuted by **Christians** who blamed them for killing Jesus. This was one reason why Jews were not allowed even to live in England for over 500 years.

The most serious persecution of Jews took place in the 1930s and '40s, when the Nazis were in power in Germany. Their leader was Adolf Hitler, and he hated the Jews. Dislike because of race or religion is called **prejudice**. Hitler was totally prejudiced against Jews, and he set out to destroy them completely. Little by little, all the Jews' rights were taken away. First, all Jews had to register at a local office. Then they were not allowed to go outside unless they were wearing a badge with the Star of David on it, so that they could be recognized in the street. No one was allowed to buy things from Jewish shops. Jews were not allowed to own cars or use buses or trains. Children were not allowed to go to school. Jews were not allowed to be

Jews in Nazi Germany had to wear a Star of David badge

outside after 9 p.m. ... The list went on and on. Then the Nazis introduced what they called the 'final solution to the Jewish problem'. Special camps were organized, and Jews were rounded up like animals. Some were killed at once. Others were starved, not allowed enough clothes, and had their hair shaved off. Torture was common, and every day thousands were sent to the gas chambers.

By the end of World War II, one in every three Jews in the world had been killed. Six million Jews, one and a half million of them children, were dead. This is too many to imagine, but think of it as equal to one in nine people in the British Isles today.

It is important to ask how this could happen. Most of the people who mistreated the Jews were more or less 'normal'. They acted as they did because Hitler managed to persuade them that Jews were not human. He said they were animals, who were responsible for all the many problems which Germany had at that time. This is called making someone a **scapegoat** – blaming them for something which is not their fault. Many people in Germany were ready to make the Jews scapegoats for all their problems, and so the Jews were persecuted.

The awful suffering which they have gone through helps to explain why many Jews today are very aware of their 'Jewishness'. It also explains why family life is so important.

> 'First they came for the Jews
> and I did not speak out –
> because I was not a Jew.
> Then they came for the communists
> and I did not speak out –
> because I was not a communist.
> Then they came for the trade
> unionists and I did not speak out –
> because I was not a trade unionist.
>
> Then they came for me –
> and there was no one left
> to speak out for me.'

These words were written by Pastor Niemoller, a victim of the Nazis

This sculpture is part of the memorial at Yad Vashem to Jews killed by the Nazis

New words

Christian follower of Jesus
Persecution ill-treatment because of religion etc.
Prejudice unjustified dislike, often based on race or religion
Scapegoat person made to take blame for others

Anne Frank

Anne Frank was a Jewish girl whose family went into hiding from the Nazis in Holland. This is part of what she wrote in her diary on 19 November 1942.

> *Countless friends and acquaintances have gone to a terrible fate. Evening after evening, the grey and green army lorries trundle past. The Germans ring at every front door and inquire if there are any Jews living in the house. If there are any, the whole family has to go at once. If they don't find any, they go on to the next house. No one has a chance of evading them unless they go into hiding. Often they go round with lists, and only ring when they know they can get a good haul. ... In the evenings when it's dark, I often see rows of good, innocent people accompanied by crying children, walking on and on, in charge of a couple of these chaps, bullied and knocked about until they almost drop. No one is spared – old people, babies, expectant mothers, the sick – each and all join in the march of death. And all because they are Jews!*

Modern Jewish history

This section tells you about recent Jewish history.

The Jews 'home-land' is called Israel. Israel is a Hebrew word which means 'fighter for God'. Israel includes more or less the same area of land as Canaan, the country which Jews believe God gave to Abraham.

After World War II, many people in the world felt that Jews should have a country where they would be safe from persecution. Many Jews had gone to live there, and many more were **refugees** who wanted to go there. Israel was finally made a separate country in 1948. The law of Israel says that any Jew has the right to go and live there if they wish.

The Arab countries which are Israel's neighbours were very angry that the land had been given to the Jews. Arabs had lived there for hundreds of years, and they felt that the land should stay Arab. Jews feel that the land is theirs, because God promised it to Abraham and Jews lived there long before the first Arab settled there.

The Western wall is an important place of pilgrimage

The position of Israel

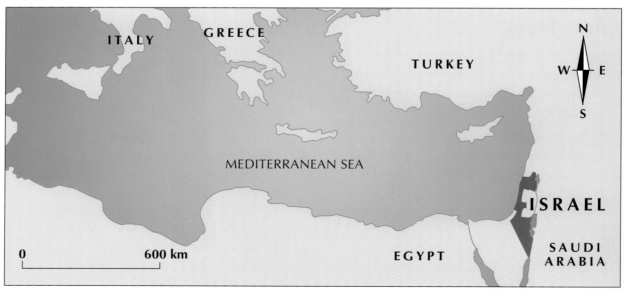

Soon after Israel became a separate country, Arab armies attacked it because their leaders thought that the state should not be allowed to exist. There were major wars between Jews and Arabs in 1956, 1967 and 1973. Although there have been suggestions for solving the disagreements, none has been accepted by all sides. This is the reason for much of the trouble in the Middle East today. There are still many problems along the borders of Israel, as countries fight over areas of land which they both claim should belong to them.

One reason why there is so much bitterness is that the area is very important for religious reasons. Jews, Christians and **Muslims** all have important events in their religious history which took place in Jerusalem, the capital city. This has been fought over for hundreds of years. It has now been divided. In 1967, Jews captured East Jerusalem, which includes the site of the Temple. The Temple was the holiest place in the Jewish religion. It was destroyed by the Romans in 70 CE. All that remains today is the Western Wall. This is an important place of **pilgrimage** for Jews, who go there to pray.

This model shows what the Temple in Jerusalem looked like

New words

Muslim follower of the religion of Islam

Pilgrimage journey made for religious reasons

Refugee person who has no nationality

Israel's Declaration of Independence

This is part of the Declaration of Independence of the State of Israel. It was read out on 14 May 1948.

We, the members of the National Council, representing the Jewish people in the Land of Israel, do hereby proclaim the establishment of a Jewish State in the Land of Israel.

The State of Israel will be open to Jewish immigration and the ingathering of exiles. It will devote itself to developing the land for the good of all its inhabitants. It will rest upon the foundations of liberty, justice and peace as envisioned by the prophets of Israel. It will maintain complete equality of social and political rights for all its citizens, without distinction of creed, race or sex. It will guarantee freedom of religion and conscience, of language, education and culture. It will safeguard the Holy Place of all religions. It will be loyal to the principles of the United Nations Charter.

Judaism today

This section tells you about Jewish groups in the world today.

All followers of all religions are individual men and women, and of course they do not all have exactly the same ideas about their beliefs. Some people may think that one part of the religion is more important than another, and so on. Followers of Judaism all share belief in its basic teachings, but different groups of Jews do not agree about other parts of the religion and about how they should live their lives.

The main groups of Jews in the world today are Orthodox Jews, Reform Jews and Liberal Jews. More Jews are Orthodox than Reform or Liberal – over 75 per cent of Jews living in the UK today are Orthodox, although not all of them are 'strict' Orthodox.

Orthodox Jews studying the scriptures

Orthodox Jews

Orthodox Jews believe that traditional ways of observing their religion are important. They keep the traditional laws of Judaism more strictly than other Jews. They believe that the Torah is the word of God, and shows how God wants people to live. The Torah will never

Inside a Reform synagogue

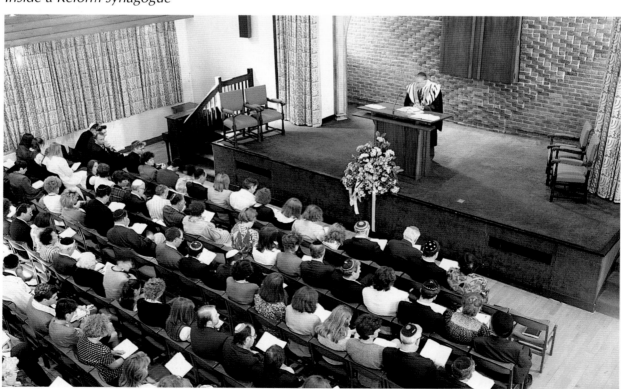

change although, as times change, the teachings may be applied in different ways, so that people can know what God wants whenever and wherever they live.

Reform and Liberal Jews

Reform and Liberal Jews are not the same, but they share the belief that Judaism can change to fit different circumstances. The changes usually make it easier to live among people who are not Jews. For example, Reform and Liberal Jews do not keep the laws of the Torah as strictly as Orthodox Jews. They believe that laws can be changed or forgotten if they no longer seem to be useful. Orthodox Jews do not agree with these teachings.

In the synagogue

In an Orthodox synagogue, men and women sit separately. In Reform and Liberal synagogues, they sit together, and men do not always wear a kippah. In Orthodox services,

women do not take part except as members of the **congregation**. In Reform synagogues, women also take part in leading the services, and may become rabbis.

In Orthodox synagogues, the services are always held in Hebrew, although prayer books also have the prayers printed in English. In Reform and Liberal synagogues, prayers are more likely to be said in English. Orthodox services on the Sabbath and at festivals do not use musical instruments, but Reform synagogues often use organs. The way in which Sabbath and festivals are observed is also different.

New word

Congregation group of people meeting for worship

Psalm 121

This psalm includes statements about God which all Jews believe.

A song for the choir standing on the Temple stairs

I will lift up my eyes to the mountains,
Where will my help come from?
My help will come from the Lord,
who makes heaven and earth.
He will not let your foot slip,
Your Guardian will not doze.
See, the Guardian of Israel

will not doze or sleep.
The Lord is your protector;
the Lord is your shade
on the right hand.
By day the sun will not strike you,
nor the moon by night.
The Lord will guard you from all harm.
He will protect your life.
The Lord will protect your comings and
* goings*
from now and for ever more.

Judaism in the home

This section tells you something about how Jews keep their religion at home.

Judaism is not just a set of beliefs, it is a way of life. The way in which Jews dress, eat and live are important parts of following their religion. This section looks at two of many different ways in which Jews carry out their beliefs at home.

Mezuzahs

A **mezuzah** is a tiny scroll made of parchment. It has the prayer called the Shema written on it. The scroll is covered by a box which may be made of wood, plastic or metal. This is to protect the scroll. The box is fastened to the right-hand side of every doorpost, except doors to the bathroom and toilet. On their way in or out of the room, strict Jews touch the box. It reminds them that God is present in the house.

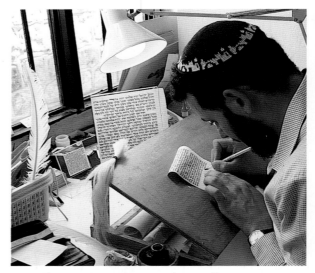

A scribe writing a mezuzah scroll

Food

Judaism has laws about which foods may be eaten, and how food should be prepared. Strict Jews keep these laws very carefully. Most Jews keep at least some of the laws. Jewish food shops and more and more supermarkets sell food which has been manufactured so that it obeys Jewish food laws.

Food which Jews are allowed to eat is called **kosher**. All plants are kosher, but not all fish and animals are. The list of foods which are allowed is found in the book of Leviticus. Animals which chew the cud and have hooves which are split (for example cows and sheep) are kosher. Animals which do not (for example pigs and rabbits) are not kosher. Fish are allowed if they have fins and scales, but shellfish are not. Any animal which is to be eaten must be killed in a special way. Before being cooked, the meat is soaked in cold water and sprinkled with salt. This removes all the blood from it. A kosher butcher may prepare the meat so that it is ready to be cooked.

A mezuzah

The foods on the left are kosher, those on the right are not

The laws say that meat and dairy foods cannot be eaten together, so for example, butter will not be used in a meat sandwich, nor will milk or cream sauces be eaten with meat.

Jews usually wait at least three hours before 'mixing' meat and milk, so a pudding with custard or cream, or coffee with milk, would not follow a meat course. To keep meat and milk totally separate, many Jewish kitchens have two sets of crockery, cutlery and tea-cloths. They also have two sinks or two bowls, so that the two sets can be washed separately.

For Jews, preparing food carefully and eating it are ways of worshipping God, because God has given the food. For the same reason, they thank him before and after meals.

New words

kosher 'fit' – food which Jews can eat
mezuzah tiny scroll of the Shema

Birkot hamazon

This is the beginning of the grace which is said after meals. Birkot hamazon means 'blessings for food'.

You are blessed, Lord our God, King of the Universe, who feeds the whole world with your goodness, with grace, kindness and compassion. He gives food to all living things, for his kindness is eternal. And in his great goodness food has never failed us, nor will it fail us forever, for the sake of his great name. For he feeds us and sustains everything and does good with every being, and prepares food for all his creatures which he has created. You are blessed, Lord, who provides food for all.

Special occasions I

This section tells you about the special things which happen to Jewish children.

Babies

Jewish babies are always given a special Hebrew name, which is often chosen to remember a relation. This name is used as well as their 'ordinary' name, and it will always be used at important religious ceremonies.

Circumcision

Healthy Jewish baby boys are **circumcised** on the eighth day after birth. (If a baby is ill, he will not be circumcised until he is well.) Circumcision means removing the foreskin, the flap of skin at the end of the penis. It is quite a common operation. Circumcision may be done by a doctor, or by a rabbi who is specially trained. A boy is given his name during this ceremony, which often takes place after morning prayers at the synagogue. Baby girls are given their names in the synagogue on the Sabbath after their birth.

Bar Mitzvah

A Jewish boy becomes Bar Mitzvah at the age of thirteen. Bar Mitzvah means 'son of the commandments'. On the Sabbath after his thirteenth birthday, a boy recites the blessing on the Torah before it is read in the synagogue.

A Bar Mitzvah ceremony in a synagogue in Jerusalem

This Bat Mitzvah girl is holding a copy of the Scriptures which she has decorated

Some boys may read the passage from the Torah, too. He must have practised the Hebrew well enough to be able to read it in public. Friends and relatives will often come to the service, and there may be a celebration meal afterwards.

Once he has reached the age of Bar Mitzvah, a Jewish boy is counted as a man. He can be one of the ten men necessary before a synagogue service can be held, and he is expected to obey all the Jewish laws.

Bat Mitzvah

A girl becomes Bat Mitzvah automatically at the age of twelve. Bat Mitzvah mean 'daughter of the commandments'. Not all Orthodox synagogues have special services to celebrate Bat Mitzvahs. If they do, they are held on a Sunday rather than the Sabbath. Girls do not read from the Torah in an Orthodox synagogue. In a Reform synagogue, there is no difference between the services held for boys and girls. A party for family and friends is usually held after the service.

New word

Circumcision removal of the foreskin

A prayer for Bar Mitzvah

This is part of the prayer which a boy says at his Bar Mitzvah in a Reform synagogue.

May I be a true Bar Mitzvah, son of the commandments, taking my place in the community of Israel, accepting its responsibilities, rejoicing in its blessing. May I be a witness to the living God and his goodness, and the tradition that lives within me.

I remember all those who have helped me to reach this time. I give thanks for the love and care of my family, the patience and instruction of my teachers, and the support and companionship of my friends.

In the Torah I have read the word of God. With your help may I go on to fulfil it in my life. Amen.

Special occasions II

This section tells you about what happens at special events in a Jew's life.

Marriage

Jews have always thought that it is important to be married. Usually, a Jew is expected to marry a Jew, because it is thought that it will be difficult to have a happy life with someone who does not understand and share their faith. A Jewish wedding service is conducted by a rabbi. Most take place in the synagogue, although they can be held in other places. Wherever the service is held, the bride and groom always stand under a special canopy. This is called a **huppah**. It is a symbol of the home which the couple will share. It is often decorated with flowers.

The couple drink from a glass of wine which has had a blessing said over it. The marriage contract is read and signed by the bridegroom. This says that the husband will look after his wife. Then the bridegroom gives the bride a ring, which she wears on the forefinger of her right hand. At the end of the service, the groom crushes a glass under his foot. (It is wrapped for safety.) No one really knows where or why this custom began, but it reminds the couple that there will be bad things as well as good in their married life, and they must face

The bride and groom stand under the huppah

Jewish graves

New words

Cremation burning a body after death
Huppah canopy used for wedding
ceremony

them together. It is also a reminder that the Temple in Jerusalem – the holiest place for Jews – was destroyed.

Divorce

Jews allow couples to divorce, but there are usually great efforts to save a marriage. Friends and relatives will do their best to help the couple to sort out their problems. If divorce cannot be avoided, the husband gives the wife a certificate of divorce. This is the only way a Jewish marriage can be ended. Jewish law then allows a person to remarry.

Death

Jews believe that funerals should take place as soon as possible after someone has died. If possible, it should be within 24 hours. Funeral services are always very simple. Jews believe that there should be no difference between rich and poor, because death happens to everyone. Most Jews do not allow bodies to be **cremated**, because they think that it destroys what God has made.

After death

Jews do believe in a life after death, but it is not a very important part of their faith. They believe that it is more important to concentrate on this life, rather than think about what might happen in a future life.

Psalm 100

This psalm is read at Jewish weddings.

A psalm of thanksgiving

Shout out to the Lord, all the earth!
Serve the Lord in happiness!
Come before him with shouts of joy!
Know that the Lord is God.
He made us, and we are his –
his people and the sheep of his
  pasture.
Come into his gates with
  thanksgiving,
into his courtyards with praises!
Thank him, bless his name.
For the Lord is good
and his kindness is eternal;
and his faithfulness is from
  generation to generation.

Index

The numbers in **bold** tell
where the main definitions
of the words are.